"HOW DARE YOU!"
Insidious
Ways
Women
Are
(Mis)treated

"HOW DARE YOU!"
Insidious
Ways
Women
Are
(Mis)treated

The #MeToo Movement:
A Memoir, Experiences of Others
and How to Heal

Lucy Papillon Ph.D.

ARCHWAY
PUBLISHING

Archway Publishing books may be ordered through booksellers or by contacting:

Archway Publishing
1663 Liberty Drive
Bloomington, IN 47403
www.archwaypublishing.com
1 (888) 242-5904

COVER PHOTO:
Shaun Lang
www.ShaunLang.com

ISBN: 978-1-4808-7181-6 (sc)
ISBN: 978-1-4808-7179-3 (hc)
ISBN: 978-1-4808-7180-9 (e)

Library of Congress Control Number: 2018914654

Print information available on the last page.

Archway Publishing rev. date: 1/17/2019

I dedicate this book to a very giving, kind and multi-talented man, Ben Caswell, who was indispensable during the process of writing this book. He often edited the manuscript alongside me before we sent it to the team of editors. He also brought a fresh look and new set of eyes to the book, which was always beneficial to me. I am extremely blessed because he is also my beloved son.

CONTENTS

CHAPTER 1

You've Got a Lot of Nerve

I want my stuff back ...
stealing my shit
from me
don't make it yours
makes it stolen ...
and it wasn't a
spirit took my
stuff
was a (man)
I made too much room for.
Ntozake Shange

ONE SUNDAY MORNING, a seven-year-old
waited in line forty-five minutes in order to speak
to the senior pastor of a huge downtown church in

a large city. This minister, when the little girl got to him, said, in an angry voice, "What are *you* doing here?" I was that little girl, and it was one of the many abusive experiences I had growing up. Since my father never seemed to have time for me, I had thought that maybe, just maybe, he would give me attention in this line. He was giving attention to all the other people who had come to the service and were in line that morning. I was wrong.

I am sharing a little of my story because my experience is directly related to the #MeToo movement. I picked the word *insidious* to describe the remarks and behaviors of so many people in my life (and perhaps yours). It captures those behaviors that are not in keeping with accepted standards of what is right, as well as contrary to our values and welfare. My parents were both distant and very mean to me the entire time I lived at home and even when I left to go to graduate school. My mother was threatened by me; she knew my father had been sexually inappropriate with me, though she had no proof of that. I remember he had been exposing himself one day; his bathroom was right next to my bedroom, so it was not difficult for this unthinkable behavior to occur without anyone else knowing about it.

Because my father was a well-known minister, I was introduced to ministers all the time. His associate would come over to me almost every Sunday and say inappropriate words to me, hugging me too tight and for too long. Then he would walk away (thinking I probably liked it; I didn't). Another minister often did the same thing—hug me too long and too tightly, saying words I was offended by. He too would then walk away. In another church I went to when my father was out of town for a preaching engagement, I got to know the preacher. When I would go up to him to tell him I liked his sermon, he would grab me and hug me very tightly, pushing his pelvis into mine. It was repulsive to me, but I had no idea what to say to stop this type of sexual mistreatment at that time in my life.

The most insidious incident of a minister's behavior was perpetrated by one of the most well-known preachers in California. He was very progressive in general, liberal in his sermons. He knew me because I attended his church quite often when I visited California, and one Sunday he invited me to dinner at his hotel. He said, "When you get there, just call my room." I did. He then said on the house phone, "Come on up and meet me; then we can go to dinner." I trusted this man; he was well respected in every circle I knew.

I went to his room. He opened the door in a silk bathrobe, open in the front, with nothing else on. I was completely numb, unable to move or run. I actually didn't know what to do. I walked in (not a smart idea), and he began by asking me to sit on his lap. I didn't, and he became forceful at that point. I somehow moved to the door and said I'd meet him at the restaurant, opened that door quickly, and started running to the elevator.

The meal was quiet, to put it mildly, and soon

over. I couldn't sleep that evening, wondering if there were any other things I might have done to avoid the awful experience. I never could think of any. I was sick to my stomach before morning and got an earlier flight out of town.

When I received my Ph.D., I had to give myself a celebration dinner. No one else offered. I invited my parents, and they brought a box of stationery they had bought at the local pharmacy. Mother had bought it as one more way of hurting me, singling me out as someone she didn't like, and even said to me often, "You are a moody, negative, unloving, and unlovable daughter," while she praised the other three siblings. They were bright lights in her life.

One time I told a close family friend my experiences (excluding the blatant sexual experience by my father), and she stated, "Oh, they are wonderful. You are just exaggerating for attention. They are great parents; you should be thankful you have them."

I felt like this denial was more mistreatment. My brothers just avoided me.

One incident that stands out for me as emblematic of the need for a #MeToo movement came when I applied to the Ph.D. program in clinical psychology. I had never made a B in my life, not in high school, college, (getting the honor of Phi Beta Kappa as a junior), or my master's program. When I got a rejection letter, not only was I shocked, but I couldn't make sense of it. I was very dejected as I walked through the halls of the school, and a male friend (that's important; I wonder if a woman would have suggested this idea) said to me in a strong voice, "Go in there right now and ask the director why you were rejected. Point out to him your grade-point average and other extracurricular activities as reasons you imagined you had a good chance of being accepted into the program."

I was very hesitant, not used to asking authority figures questions like that, but I did it. The director said to me, "I know with your being very attractive [intimating "sexy" by the way he said the word] and all the doors that have opened because of it, you have gotten everything on a silver platter, and I, plus the committee [all males, I found out later], decided that we weren't going to perpetuate that by admitting you into the program."

Even before I could be stunned, I burst into tears, crying hard. When I could finally speak, I said, "It has been the opposite for me. I have had to work extremely hard for every single thing I have ever gotten. You have no idea what I have been through in my life to get to this point."

He looked sheepish and embarrassed. He had been caught in an assumption so many men make about women, whether it is being accepted into a program, getting a job, requesting a raise, or anything else. It is part of that "boys' club" mentality. Yes, it is insidious; that's why so many women are now standing up against it.

My experience in the selection process of the doctoral program – while not sexual assault – revealed that I was never even *seen* beyond my appearance. While not an assault physically, it certainly felt demeaning, demoralizing, and disempowering to learn that I was not valued beyond objectification in the male gaze.

It is telling that 38 years later, women who come forward with accusations of sexual assault are not just disbelieved, but somehow asked for the abuse because of the way we look, dress or behave. Yes, it is heartening to see the rise of both the #MeToo and the #whyIdidnotreport social movements (the latter in direct response to the mentality and ridiculous assertions by mostly white men that the victims of sexual assault are not only to be blamed for the abuse itself but also for not speaking up sooner).

Sexual trauma is different from having your car stolen. It is not a crime like that. The damage of sexual assault is such that victims can't simply call the police and point to where the car was parked. Because it is a psychic wound, it is easier to deny that it happened at all – both for the victim and for the perpetrator. Often there is no evidence. And if the victim questions whether it happened (for any number of reasons, including disassociation, embarrassment, shame/guilt, or denial), then reporting it right away becomes much less likely. It takes years for some to find their own voice around sexual assault, if at all. And perpetrators of this type of misuse of sexual power can deny their culpability forever.

Let me just say, before I finish telling you my own experience, that I have finally found a place in the world where I feel totally accepted, totally embraced, and absolutely never judged about anything concerning me: Italy. I have been going to the same two places there now for seven years. People are always asking me, why don't you go to Ireland, England, etc., and I say, "I have no desire to go anywhere except these two places." I don't feel the need to explain my choice to them. One is a villa on the Amalfi Coast; the other is a wonderful hotel in central Florence. They all welcome me back and treat me as if I am a very special human being. In fact, the family who owns the villa says now, "You are part of our family."

Fortunately, it is far different from the family I grew up in. My Italian family treats me as if I am a treasure, a great person, one they want to be around. I am thrilled. It is not something I have felt in my life. Do you have a place where you can go to feel that special warmth and acceptance? If not, start your search; you will surely find it.

> We can't pick and choose based on whose ... beliefs we believe in. and that means we have to be willing to speak out when it's a member of our own (family).
> **Sara Gelser, state senator**
> **a Silence Breaker, one of**
> **the voices that launched the**
> **#MeToo movement**

CHAPTER 2

If These Walls Could Speak

I said to my soul, be still, and wait
without hope
For hope would be hope for the
wrong thing; wait without love
For love would be love of the wrong
thing; there is yet faith
But the faith and love and the hope
are all in the waiting.
Wait without thought, for you are not
ready for thought:
So the darkness shall be the light,
and the stillness the dancing.
T. S. Eliot

NOW I WANT to turn to the many patient stories I have heard over my years in practice. The one that was the most painful to hear, even as she spoke about it the first day, concerns a thirty-eight-year-old woman, married to one of the most sexually abusive men I have ever heard about from patients. The most poignant example of her experience was when she had cancer and was pregnant with her son. She was in the hospital, getting chemotherapy, and her husband came into the room. He pulled her halfway off the bed and began to rape her. She screamed for him to stop, but he didn't. He never stopped; he did it every day she was married to him. She commented to me that he told her, "I have to have it every day, or I can't work." She was sobbing as she reported the story to me. She still has terrible post-traumatic stress from the many incidents she endured by this man. Just recently, she went to court to get the restraining order renewed, and she told me the next week, "Dr. Papillon, the judge knew; she could just tell that he was a man

I needed to stay away from and certainly one who needed to be far away from me. She gave me a restraining order that is for over ten years." I, of course, was thrilled for her.

Another patient replied to me immediately, when I asked her how her grade school sexual abuse was affecting her life today, "As you know, for a long time I couldn't go out into the world, with all those men around. Now, because I live in Germany and have to spend a lot of time out getting groceries and other things, I don't leave the flat unless I state strongly and continuously to myself, 'I am a tough bitch.'" She said she imagined the energy she felt as she put out that message could literally be felt when she walked around.

She continued, "That gave me the confidence to proceed to wherever my destination was." The statement startled me because it was completely incongruent with her quiet, subdued, and often silent personality.

Another patient in her fifties told me that, since

her husband doesn't trust her, even though she has never cheated on him, he will not allow her to go anywhere without him. He is a "bully," she said, and refuses to let her out of his sight. Before she married him, she had been an executive of a large financial firm. I could perceive, if I looked carefully, that powerful side of her. It had almost been snuffed out by his constant harassment, but glimpses of it came through every now and then throughout the sessions. I am now working with her to have her get back in touch with that part of herself. Since I know it is there and that this power can flourish, even completely change the dynamics of the relationship, I am sure she will begin to feel more empowered to speak up and speak out against this type of insidious behavior by him.

The first patient I ever treated, when I was an intern on a college campus, came into the office but barely spoke the entire time. She just looked at me, tears coming out of her eyes. She was noticeably shaking. We made an appointment for later that same week, and she slowly walked into the room. She said, "I am very ashamed to tell you anything about my past. I have never told anyone and vowed I would never ever let out my secret, but it is beginning to consume my life." I told her I was not here to judge her or condemn her, and telling me what happened could free her from the immense pain she felt. She said, "I have been carrying this extreme anguish for many years. I thought it would lessen, but it has grown worse." Then she began to explain that she was Catholic, and her brother's sexual abuse had left her with great guilt. She blamed herself and searched and searched for ways she could have brought this horrible act on. She never could. Of course she never could, because it was not her fault; it was not anything she did or didn't do that caused her brother to defile her in this way.

She replied, "But my church says we are to feel guilt for the behaviors we have done in our lives." That statement brought on a series of sessions dealing with what she had been taught and used against herself and what other ways were open to her to view this huge, damaging sexual abuse she had endured.

A much more recent example of the damage sexual abuse can do to a person came from a patient in his early sixties. He had been in therapy for several months when he began to tell me his history of sexual experiences. There were very few, actually only two, one very recent. The first was an extremely damaging one where he was raped and could not bring himself to go near a sexual encounter again. He buried himself in work and began to feel more and more terrified to try another relationship, much less a sexual one. He talked himself into thinking it was unimportant and he could just bury any desires (there were only a few that emerged) and work his way up until he was head of his department. He did become very successful and was, in my view, proud of the way he could bury those terrifying feelings about sex and lose himself in his work.

He came into my office only because, almost accidentally, he was at a party on New Year's Eve, and someone kissed him at midnight in a surprising way. It unnerved but intrigued him. Now he had to directly confront his long-held fears. He was courageous enough to step through my office door (after delaying it and trying to talk himself out of it for four months), and the work could begin.

Another poignant example of how damaging sexual abuse can be is captured in a group setting at an inpatient eating-disorder program where I was the chief psychologist. One day in the session, one of the women began to speak about her huge struggle with eating. She told the group that it started back at home in middle school. Her stepfather had exposed himself to her several times late at night. He'd come in, wake her with no clothes on, climb into her bed, and begin to rub himself against her body. She was paralyzed with both fear and concern about how she would escape from this horrible routine of his. She started to cry, and as the group went on, I asked the members how many had experienced sexually inappropriate behavior as a child. Several raised their hand (seven out of the ten in the group).

Then I asked how many of them took showers with their fathers when they were six or seven years old. All raised their hand; I continued to say that, at that age, if they can remember, their eyes were right in front of their father's genitals. I heard gasps as all realized they had had sexual mistreatment (or worse) as a young child. I also asked if their fathers had been inappropriate on any level as they went into puberty—such as popping their bras (to see if they were wearing one) or tickling them in places that were uncomfortable to them. All of them raised their hands, and that began a series of serious treatment about sexual harassment and abuse that continued for several weeks. It became clear to them why they ended up in an inpatient facility to deal with what seemed, on the surface, like "just an eating disorder."

One patient, who came in only because his wife insisted on it (she stated she would definitely divorce him otherwise), said to me, "Doctor, I don't want to be here. I don't think I have a problem. In fact, I have spoken to many friends who totally agree with me. I love my wife, though, so I am coming in, in order not to lose her. She is my best friend. We have been married for seven years now. We have three dogs but no children. The reason she is forcing me to be here is that we got into a discussion late one night, and it was about sex. We have a good sexual relationship, but I told her during this lengthy talk that no, I couldn't imagine just having sex with her, this one person, my entire life. I said that at some point, I did want to experience another woman in bed having sex. She blew up. I mean, she went into such a rage, all the dogs started barking and I imagine thought that she needed their assistance somehow. Neither one of us got much sleep that night. She was silent the next day and the next, in a sense stonewalling me by not speaking a word to me. Finally, she said, 'On only one condition will I stay in this relationship: you *must* go to therapy and soon, within a two-week period making an appointment.'"

The more this patient and I got into his issues, the more I saw that he had been quite a player before he married, experiencing all kinds of sexual encounters. He said he loved that life, and it took him a long time to get to the point where he felt he could marry someone and stay with her. Now that he was married, he said he couldn't help but touch a woman's "ass" at work, find her reaction a turn-on, and do other "naughty" (to others, not him) behaviors that aroused him. He was unable to articulate just what those harassing behaviors provided for him over time; he just knew he couldn't stop doing them.

It took many months for this man to begin to see how degrading his behavior was, not just to those women, but to his wife, who was unaware of what he was doing daily. Eventually, he uncovered a deeply held secret about several incidents early in his life where he found several sex magazines under his father's side of the bed and would look at the pictures and masturbate several times a night while reading stories about sex. He did this behavior nightly for several years and began to have sex as soon as he could find a girl in middle school to do it with him. He continued this behavior of many sexual encounters until marriage. He is still working through his many challenges with this long-held sexual acting out and more recently harassment of other women.

Another recent example of how sexual abuse at any age can affect a woman at a much later age is that of a college student who was sexually assaulted when she was five years old. Two boys who lived next door to her home abused her sexually over and over one afternoon when she was playing in her yard. They came over and invited her to play with them in their house. She agreed, trusting their motives (unfortunately). In high school, she discovered pornography, and by the time she went to college, she was completely addicted to it. By her sophomore year, she had to drop out of school; the pornography was consuming her life.

Fortunately, she searched until she found a treatment center far from home or college, where she could be totally anonymous. She spent over a month there and now is back at school but has to fight with herself not to return to the old habits that she knows were destroying the life she wants to live. She comes to sessions every week to work on the many issues that accompany any addiction. The insidious nature of sexual abuse truly does invade and often interrupt the path we are currently on to get to the goal we have set for ourselves.

Several years ago, a woman came in stating she had several panic attacks each day, at random times. Nothing she could discover was triggering these sudden experiences of panic. She used to rush to the ER because she thought she was for sure having a heart attack, but now she knows better.

She came into therapy because of isolation. She is terrified to leave the house because she may have a panic attack while driving (she will not attempt to go near a freeway anymore) or while at a party or restaurant. She has lost most of her friends because they don't understand what is going on. She is embarrassed to "expose" herself, as she puts it.

She came in because of the fear of leaving her house but also because these panic attacks are "taking over" her life. It took several months of gaining her trust and her feeling safe in my office for me to ask her if she had ever been sexually abused as a child or adolescent or at any point in her life. She burst into tears and for several minutes was unable to speak. When she did, she haltingly stated, "When I was eleven years old, my uncle came to live with us for a while. I liked him a lot, but after he'd been there a few weeks, I noticed that he would offer to hold me in his lap, even though I had told him several times I didn't want to. Finally, while my parents were gone, he took me into the bathroom, locked the door, and forced me onto the cold floor. I was numb, and while he was assaulting me sexually, I just left. "Doctor, I wasn't in that bathroom anymore. I was somewhere else; I had to be in order to survive. I can't remember now where in my head I went, but I do recall clearly that I wasn't there."

Do any of these examples of sexual abuse bring to mind long-held and deeply guarded secrets for you? If so, I urge you to go to a psychologist to move through and beyond these very painful and sometimes debilitating traumas.

> Do not be afraid of the past.
> If people tell you it is irrevocable,
> do not believe them.
> **Oscar Wilde**

CHAPTER 3

Don't Stop Believin'

We must learn to reawaken and keep
our selves awake,
not by mechanical acts
but by an infinite expectation of the
Dawn
which does not forsake us
even in our soundest sleep.
Henry David Thoreau

IN THE SOCIAL media realm, actor Alyssa Milano tweeted, "If you've been sexually harassed or assaulted, write 'me too' as a reply to this tweet" and went to sleep. The next morning, she woke up to find that fifty-five thousand people had used #MeToo. Milano burst into tears. One poet,

Najwa Zebian, wrote: "I was blamed for it, I was told it wasn't that bad, I was told to get over it."

Since I grew up among ministers, I too minimized, in my mind, what they were doing as they hugged me too tightly, some pushing their pelvis against mine. It just didn't register how insidious this behavior really was. I was used to being dealt with as an object, as a means to an end, as a woman with no power. They (whoever *they* were) had the ultimate say over me. That's the way it was in story after story, as I researched this subject. We really were under the grip of the old-boy culture. If you, as a woman, don't sense you have power over the story that dominates your life or even the audience that might listen and believe you, then you really do feel powerless, because you can't turn to anyone you think will fully believe you, and you certainly haven't got the power to think about the experiences in any new way. You feel stuck in your story, stuck in the mire of what seems to be your fate.

But now you are no longer alone. The *Time*

magazine article, naming the "Silence Breakers" as the person of the year, provides you with a group who absolutely know what you are experiencing, perhaps every day in your workplace, certainly in your life. Something really empowering is happening when people begin standing up for what is right. As great social change nearly always does, it begins with individual acts of bravery.

In truth, it began with the actions of the several women who began using #MeToo, which now has been used millions of times in at least eighty-five countries. That is truly astounding to me. Is it to you?

Finally now, these women all over the world are waking up to the fact that this trauma they have been or are experiencing is not just their story but a story shared by thousands, perhaps millions of women, some who speak up, others who just hear television and radio accounts. Nevertheless, however they begin to awaken, it is critical that they (and maybe you) do so, in order to begin to have hegemony over their (and your) own life. Where some journalists have failed, some have actually picked up what district attorneys have also failed to report, stating the truth about the sexual harassment that has been occurring for many years.

There is, of course, much we still don't know about what the final impact will be for all of these women who do choose to speak up. However, they are not about to stop speaking out against this atrocity. The biggest test of this movement will be the extent to which the movement changes the realities of the people for whom telling their truths is threatening. So many in the movement say that they want to be an example of what it means to stand up for oneself, even though they may feel the world around them is not supporting that stance.

Giving voice to the secrets so many of us (including me) have experienced, showing scores of people in social media that what is needed is to push forward—this is what is needed for all of us to stop accepting the unacceptable. Anyone who speaks their truth opens the door wider for us to enter into dialogue about it all.

For me, it was and is the most important step I can take—to tell my own story (to myself first and secondly to others)—to open up the dialogue so long held in silence, almost strangling me in that act of doing so.

Jack Saul, a psychologist and head of the trauma program in New York, stated in a piece in *Vanity Fair* that collective trauma refers to the shared injuries to a population's social ecology due to a major catastrophe or chronic oppression, poverty, and disease. While #MeToo doesn't fit neatly into this definition (according to this article by Bethany McClean), the movement may be leading to some of the features we often associate with collective traumas, social rupturing, and a profound sense of distress, the challenging of long-held assumptions about the world and national identity, a constricted public narrative, and a process of scapegoating and dehumanization. Until recently, "thanks to

Harvey Weinstein" (McClean states), historians hadn't had a perspective to fully process and acknowledge the shame #MeToo brings up. This is an important point that Bethany McClean makes here, because that is and will be a major contribution of this movement for all of the women who have been mistreated, misused, and abused by a huge number of men, especially in places of authority and power.

Of course, the journey isn't over; we must reform the way we see ourselves in this culture and be willing to take on the authority, the power, and the ongoing examination of who we choose to be, instead of where we've allowed ourselves (and society has told us) we must be. As McClean puts it so well, "we must continue to untangle the complexities and rampant nature of these insidious series of incidents [and] … must eventually come to a systemic transformation in this realm."

Over the years, I have noticed that so many people, especially my patients I have seen over a

period of time, fall into what Freud termed "repeti-
tion compulsion" as they move through their lives.
They attempt to replicate what they experienced
from their childhood traumas and think, if they
pick this person (a man, usually), they can prove
to themselves that this time they will get the experience to come out as they would have wanted it
to, way back in their childhoods. *This man I choose
won't mistreat me, sexually abuse me, but rather respect and honor me.* It never works, but since they
don't consciously realize what they are doing, they
continue to pick and stay with these abusive, unavailable, and power-hungry men who only want
to boss them, sexually abuse them, and certainly
not treasure them, as they deserve.

Haruki Murakami, considered an unofficial lau-
reate of Japan, wrote: "When you come out of the
storm, you won't be the same person who walked
in." What a powerful statement for all women:
Who were we before? Who can we be now? Are
we willing to take that first important step in the

direction of hegemony over our own lives, without needing anyone's approval or permission?

When I was doing my internship at a California university counseling center, I experienced great neglect and abuse by the other five interns during that year. They had parties without me, ignored me during meetings, said things behind my back that I would discover later, even physically moved further away when I would be in their presence. I am sharing this experience because it isn't always someone with power over us, someone who can give us a job, or a partner who can sexually abuse us, withhold money or affection from us, or disrespect us. Sometimes it is our peers who insult us, ignore us, belittle us, or try to make us feel "less than." I finally spoke to the supervisor over all of us (a very wise, respected man who was the head of the Psychology Board for the State of California at the time). He said to me when I told him about my painful experiences, "This behavior is about jealousy; it is about your finishing your dissertation when they haven't even started theirs, about your already getting a position, having been appointed to the medical school faculty."

It made a huge difference to me to understand where this set of behaviors came from, but more often than not, we don't have an opportunity to find out why someone is acting in a particular way. Sometimes I've found out through my research that women don't even think it is unusual or out of the ordinary (because it hasn't been), so they take it and often feel awful because of it, with no understanding at all of what it is about or where it came from.

I especially like what actress Ashley Judd said: "We need to formalize the whisper network. It's an ingenious way that we've tried to feel safe. All those voices can be amplified. That's my advice to women. That and if something feels wrong, it *is* wrong—and it's wrong by my definition and not necessarily anyone else's."

In the research I did, I found that many women

said there is no place to go to report their sexual harassment or assault. Even Ashley Judd stated that there wasn't a place for actors to report these horrific experiences. The #MeToo movement has certainly provided an umbrella of solidarity for these millions of women when they need and want to speak up with their stories, to me, to social media, to anyone who will listen.

Clearly, this movement has come to light now, but for centuries, it seems, women have had issues with their bosses who not only cross boundaries but don't even know that there *are* any boundaries. Finally, women have had it with the fear of retaliation, of being blackballed, of being fired from a job they can't afford to lose. But at the same time, they are "done" with men who use their power to take what they want from women. That, for me, is such a true statement because of all the experiences I've had, especially with ministers, who took what they wanted from me and gave me humiliation in return. I have plenty of anger about that and the way

I was treated since childhood. It is very comforting to note that a collective anger has emerged that has sent CEOs flying off their jobs and left many others disgraced. It is a long time coming, but finally the movement has begun. I have no sense that it is going to stop—not now, not ever, unless many changes occur in society.

Sexual harassment does bring shame. And the more we shine a light on these behaviors, the faster transformation can happen. The simple but not easy act of speaking up empowers others to share long-held secrets. The stories are eerily similar. I am not surprised, really, because we have all, if we have been among society, among powerful men, or at least men in places of power, been exposed to behaviors that are indeed repulsive to us but have silenced us in the past out of fear, shame, or other unjust but pervasive feelings. Many times, we—I know I—have blamed ourselves. Did I somehow bring this on? Am I to blame for this horrid behavior? Should I feel shame and guilt or not? Of course, it is a toxic way to think, but it is difficult, given the way we, as women, were raised, not to think and feel some of these thoughts.

A common theme among patients who are struggling or unwilling to share is a paralyzing fear that they have done something wrong and are to blame. I myself felt this way for years, even with the interns. What could *they* have possibly done wrong, I thought? I didn't know, but I wasn't willing to find out at the time.

Often, people I found through my research noticed that the very job they thought was a dream job actually turned out to be a nightmare, given the horrible mistreatment they received over time. When patients or other people I talked to spoke about their experiences, they often said that eventually they just forgot about what it might cost them to speak their truths; they just wanted to say what had happened in the way it occurred, not try to guess what might happen if they did. They stated things like, "The man didn't consider any questions about the consequences when he sexually harassed me. Why should I?"

A patient who is a professor told me: "The university went into my email to try to find something to embarrass me, since I had spoken the truth. They couldn't stop me, but they could try to stop everyone from listening. But not anymore. I won't be silent. Not now. Not ever."

I agree wholeheartedly with that. I have been speaking individually to a few close friends about my own painful and deeply personal experiences, and because of this I am finally ready to come out of hiding and talk about what I – and so many others – have endured in this life. Start with a trusted friend or professional therapist. It is both horrifying and reassuring at the same time to know I'm not alone. That is the true power of the #MeToo movement. What a relief to know I am not alone, and that I needn't feel ashamed.

Singer Taylor Swift captured the spirit of this movement when confronting the defense attorney in a sexual harassment trial last year: "I'm not going to let you or your client make me feel in any way that this is my fault. I'm being blamed for the unfortunate events of his life that are a product of his decisions, not mine." Amen to that!

> You need to claim the events of your life to make yourself yours.
> **Anne-Wilson Schaef**

CHAPTER 4

The Times, They Are a-Changin'

We are the mirror
as well as the face in it.
… we are pain
and what cures pain both,
we are the sweet cold water and the jar
that pours.
Rumi

FROM MY PERSPECTIVE, no one has ever fully understood me—no one. I moved from therapist to therapist and left the last one when he so diminished the most painful trauma I'd ever experienced in my life that I couldn't stand going to him again. He said to me, "That is a story you keep telling me. It is in your past. Why do you keep saying it?"

Why? No one has ever gotten how devastating, how utterly destroying it was to me and how everything in my life died during that long period of time. My poems, speeches, books—nothing told it like it really was. There are no words strong enough. It was about a man who destroyed my life as I knew it, every part of my life—my practice, where I lived, where I could go, just everything. I tried to date other men, but they all turned out to be abusive—not on the level of this man, but I realized I had repeated my experience with my father again and again, a huge authority figure in the city but also in my life. These men were also in power and were also abusive with me in many different ways. These other men were not as extreme as the relationship that ruined a significant period of my life, but still they were similar to my father in some ways. I picked these men, especially the worst one, and stayed way too long, not only because they were men of power and influence but also because I kept hoping, with each one, that they would one day stop abusing me, stop terrorizing my life. It never happened.

I wrote a book called *When Hope Can Kill* about how we, as women, keep hoping that tomorrow things will be different—whether the man is abusive, belittling, completely unavailable, sexually harassing, assaultive, or some other extremely demeaning behavior. I found, through writing the book, that one meaning of hope is "postponed disappointment." That certainly fit what I was doing to my Soul, my Spirit; I was killing it slowly through continuing with these men. I found an old proverb that says "Hope dies last." Unfortunately, it was certainly true with me in these situations.

In a piece I heard on NPR, a group of researchers asked women when they remember first being mistreated by a man. Ninety-seven percent of the responders stated that they had been abused in some way before they finished high school. What that suggests to me is that if they have already been introduced to mistreatment, they are likely even more susceptible to think it is normal to be treated in that way. Ever since I saw Emma Gonzalez in the #NeverAgain March for our Lives on March 24, 2018, with her six-minute silence for the seventeen killed during that same length of time, I thought, what a brave seventeen-year-old, what an enormous statement she is making by *not* speaking a word. Silence at that moment was powerful. It was in front of 800,000 young people coming together over gun laws. Can #MeToo match that? Emma Gonzalez said at the end of the six minutes of silence, "We are the change." I say *they*—they are the change for the future; *we* are the *change* in the *present*.

The two people who made the documentary on MLK that aired the same weekend as this march on changing gun laws said: "We must speak up and take a stand on what we think is important. That really is critical for any real change." The documentary shows MLK saying that "we are the ones that must redeem the Soul of America." These filmmakers of the documentary also asserted: "Dr. King inspired us to get into trouble, 'good trouble,' in order to make us better able to inspire others." I think we know how much of a role Dr. King played in our getting as far as we are. We just need to keep on pushing the long-held boundaries that have stayed in place way too long. I certainly know that when we don't, we are contributing to the continuation of our own and others' mistreatment. I realize many have started speaking out, but I want to hear many more voices speak up and speak out against whatever they have experienced that they consider mistreatment of their own hegemony over their own space, body, future in a profession, whatever it is for you, for anyone.

What I have concluded, through my research, my own experiences, my patients, and so many articles I read about the #MeToo movement is: we are more susceptible to being mistreated in many ways due to many of our upbringings, where we are subtly or directly told not to speak up. Did my mother speak up? Never. Did your mother speak up? What models did you have as a child that taught you speaking up was the best thing you could do? I was punished if I dared to speak up, which of course I soon quit doing. Speaking up, I've noticed over time, did not help a woman and often got her more abuse, more demeaning behavior from whoever she chose to speak up to.

Just recently, as a small example, I was on a flight that was going to be rather lengthy. I asked the flight attendant, a young man, if he could ask the pilots to turn down the air conditioning (it was wintertime) or turn up the heat just a bit. He replied, "What's wrong with you? It's not cold on this plane." I was silenced by that remark. I regretted soon after, though, that I hadn't thought of an appropriate reply to this demeaning statement at the moment. I did turn him in to the airline's customer service though (which is certainly not as empowering as stating something to him myself). I'm still learning, I noticed. As I sat freezing during the rest of the flight, I asked myself, "What were you afraid of? What did you think might happen if you stated to the flight attendant that that statement was uncalled for, rude, and demeaning?" I wish I could say I came up with clear answers for myself at the time.

Now that I have researched this #MeToo movement more thoroughly, I can think of many answers to my own questions. For example, I can clearly remember a quote from a Silence Breaker, Lindsey Reynolds, who stated, "I sent an email to my bosses complaining of the company's culture of sexism." She then added, "After I sent it I burst into tears and felt sick at my stomach and was shaking. I was nobody. I was just a person from a small town in Texas. I have no money, no power, no social standing. I felt extremely vulnerable and scared." Fortunately for her and now for me, she said that she had heard from women she had never met who had experienced the same toxic culture. "They were line cooks and such, not in power positions."

When one grows up in a toxic environment where parents and/or siblings are demeaning, emotionally and/or physically abusive, acting as if you don't exist, you are much more susceptible to the uncalled for and unwanted abuse and mistreatment of others. It's not that it is your fault; it is that you are not used to and may not know what respectful and appropriate behavior feels and looks like. It sounds preposterous, I know, but I have seen it over and over, and people tell me that they don't have any idea what really appropriate behavior feels like. They didn't grow up with healthy, respectful experiences and are still grappling with what they are supposed to experience in a healthy relationship, for example.

When you are not treasured, you may well conclude you aren't worthy to be treasured, or you would have been. This is the setup for all kinds of abusive relationships or other kinds of mistreatment, such as in a professional environment. When you are treated as a child like you barely deserve to exist, it is not shocking when, as an adult, you are treated in a similar way. In a way, it is an insidious setup, because you really do believe you don't deserve to be treated well; you can long for attention, but you don't actually expect it. When you are taken advantage of or lose a position, an appointment as a professor or any promotion, it may be because you didn't think you were worthy of it. It could also be that the ones in charge thought you were not obeying all the rules of behavior (stated and unstated) that you had to follow in order to get that promotion. It seems very unfair, but, given the way you were raised, perhaps you didn't learn how to "read" people in a way you needed to in order to get to a higher level in your job. The environment you grew up in has such a major impact on your future experiences that it is hard to emphasize it too much.

However, that is not the end of the story for

you. You must get to the point where you begin to understand where you came from and what you learned as a child that may not now (or ever) serve you at all.

I wrote the following poem as I began to awaken, not just to one man who traumatized me by his insidious abuse, but to all men who have mistreated women for way too long.

> You know, I think you're blind
> to what you have and
> who I am:
> a flower,
> that delicate, killable
> gift of God's.
> That moment when the
> flower just opens
> to gasp for breath,
> for light, its life,
> it's crushable,
> so soft and easily broken

into scattered petals
across a stone, cold pavement.
You don't even see
that that precious fragile heart
is easily wounded,
has been stomped on.
The flower must stand
for itself,
by itself,
for enjoying,
for savoring,
certainly, for light touching.
Oh yes, gentle
gently wanting to be intact
for its whole life.
Instead, it gets holes punctured in it
as if by a madman with a shotgun.
You come.
You take.
You devour.
You shoot, shout, scream

at the flower,
kick its freshness
into a stagnant pool of
sewer water
as if it were to thrive
on dirt or vulgarities.
You never notice the
dew on each petal
are actually tears,
drowning in tears of "Stop it.
Quit the savage slaughter."
a flower, pure,
expecting room to flourish,
expecting care and love
told it is beautiful.
You see my splendor
why do you tear at my soul?
don't you know it's all
bound together,
that to beat at my outsides
is to cut at my core?

This poem endeavors to capture the insidious, toxic way we can be treated. It may have lasted so long that we aren't even conscious of just how horrid it really can be for us. We can take the precious flower at our core and allow it to be beaten up, defiled, and crushed of its beauty—with words from others, or more hideously, from their hands or weapons. It is all very damaging to us, and we must wake up to what we are allowing or what we think we may deserve. No one ever has the right to treat us in any way other than with great respect. That is our right and our obligation to ourselves as we awaken to our own preciousness within us. When is enough enough? There is only one answer—now.

CHAPTER 5

Where Have All The Flowers Gone?

The seed that is to grow
Must lose itself as seed;
And they that creep
May graduate through
Chrysalis to wings.

Wilt thou then, O mortal,
Cling to husks
Which falsely seem to you
The Self?
Wu Ming Fu

Not "Revelation" ——'tis-that waits,
But our unfurnished eyes-
Emily Dickinson

WHEN I THINK of women being mistreated, two songs immediately come to mind: *"I am woman, hear me roar"* and *"These boots are made for walking and I'm goin' to walk all over you."* These songs are the epitome of owning your power as a woman, about seeing your Self as worthy of respect, as much respect as anyone else, no matter who they are - doctor, professor, lawyer...

I was given the original picture of myself as a child, an adorable, beautiful child as I looked at it through adult eyes when finally receiving it about ten years ago. The photo won several awards as capturing the most beautiful, photogenic child. What I immediately thought when I was given the photo was - but I was never told these descriptions, I was never, ever told I was beautiful by my mother, so as a result, I felt ugly. I was never told that I was photogenic, so I hid from having my picture taken.

I told a patient to bring in a picture of himself at around 14 years old. He reluctantly did but would not look at it. He said it had been in a drawer at his home for years and he hated that child, absolutely could not stand the sight of him. He said that fourteen-year-old was disgusting. I asked what the child had done that was so horrid. He said that the child could not make his mother "act right," and when his father came home from work, he would scream at this fourteen-year-old because he hadn't obeyed him. The mother had a bi-polar disorder, but no one had diagnosed her at that time so the father just felt that the boy, my patient, was being lazy. He wasn't.

I work with my patient every week on how to be a loving, nurturing, comforting parent to that little boy inside of him. He has no model for that so it is a process he is having to learn slowly. He is starting to do a few things better around that, but, up until now, has "lost" the picture so can't bring it into therapy with him each week any longer. He has a very difficult time loving himself if he feels he's "slipped up" in any way.

When my father died, mother completely changed. It was obvious then how squelched she had been, how much he had, without saying much, stopped her from speaking up about anything. As far as the children knew, she had no opinions; she just did what he told her to do. She did not seem to have a self apart from him. Such was the era. Once he died, however, she began to blossom and realize that she did have a voice and thus choices, opinions, freedom to be. It was transformative to her and for me, as her child, to observe.

The #MeToo movement only brought to light what had been happening for years and years in small ways. It shined the light on these injustices and allowed women to say out loud (and even shout at times) "I *am* important," "I *do* have a voice," and "I *am* going to use my voice whenever I notice disrespect," or anything that I might have been too scared to speak of before. A critical mass has occurred now and we, as women, won't be stopped.

When did *you* find your voice – middle school,

college, after a divorce... or have you found it yet? Sally Field came out in September, 2018 with a memoir called "In Pieces" wherein she states that after taking six years to write the book, she finally discovered that she has a voice worthy to be heard and won't be stopped anymore from using it. The thing is, once we, as women, discover we have a voice, we do become unstoppable. Sally Field had been sexually abused for many years by her step-father but knew she wouldn't be believed so, until her mother was very ill, she had never told anyone. She said she was also abused by many men throughout her life. It was very important to her to find she had a voice so that now she can heal even more thoroughly.

We heal through speaking, not through silence. We must be accountable to ourselves for speaking up, we can't wait for men to allow it – women have to take it upon themselves to own our own voices, but not just own it, use it!

The day after Dr. Christine Blasey Ford stated

that she was sexually assaulted by the judicial nominee for the Supreme Court, Brett Kavanaugh, hundreds of thousands of women came forward talking about why they had not come forward about their own sexual violence. Many thought no one would believe them. One said "I was frozen with fear, I was twelve years old." Another said she was humiliated. She felt it might ruin her reputation even before it had been built fully. Still another said she was sure *she* would be blamed if she spoke up.

Suddenly a movement had begun (#whyididn'treport), ignited by Dr. Ford's willingness to risk her reputation, her profession and even her life (she has had many death threats and her family has had to go into hiding, relocating multiple times) in order to speak about what she felt was essential for all to know before this man was voted onto the Supreme Court for a lifetime appointment. Now #whyIdidn'tReport has grown so large it almost, in one day, shut down social media, especially the Twitter feed.

We women will no longer stay silent, we have watched another, now several others, say what they had never said out loud before. Now they will not be silenced. Critical mass has come to the world in terms of women no longer being silenced by their fears, other's threats, low sense of self-esteem, by their own distorted thinking that it was somehow their fault it happened.

This powerful movement reminds me of a Native American Proverb:

> As you go the way of life,
> You will see a great chasm.
> Jump. It is not as wide as you think.

Some of the quotes women voiced about why they had not said anything before are: "I can't make waves, so I just won't express my anger about these sexual assault incidents I've experienced;" "I must not speak up or take a stand if I ever want to be loved;" "People will say it is my fault because of the way I dress;" "My religious beliefs say, 'Turn the other cheek,' 'Pray harder,' 'Endure because it is your duty as a woman...'" Another woman said, "I am so ashamed and embarrassed that these sexual incidents happened, I've withstood so much in my life, I can withstand this too. I know I can." Still another said, "I may deserve better than this, but then, I may not. Most of the time I think I deserved every bit of the sexual assaults I've received."

One woman tweeted: "If I don't name it, it doesn't exist." Another admitted, "I don't see it as a betrayal of myself, besides, I just don't see the point of speaking up about the sexual abuse, after all, it happened a long time ago." Another example of a woman's statement: "I am a victim and have no power to change anything, including what happened (or may happen again)." Still another woman said, "It occurred so early in my life, why would I bring it up now, even though I think about it every day, it was long ago he sexually assaulted me over and over..." Another woman shared, "I have just pretended I am fine. I never believed it [that I am fine], but I think everyone else does when they meet me or even become friends with me. I have never told a soul [about my abuse] and I don't intend to start now – how would the people I now know react? I can't take that chance."

One woman said a lot about how she felt when she revealed publicly over social media: "The most insidious crimes do not end up in the criminal court buildings. The perpetrators are never tried and most offenses are repeated violations to my body. But I see it as a crime of the heart. I have suffered over the years from these terrifying experiences, I know my soul is the one being violated. No one else can see it, that is the horror of it all too, I have suffered alone. The bruises are all internal. I guessed – until now with Dr. Ford's coming into the spotlight – that it wouldn't be worth it. Now I guess it would be but what will come of her after the hearing? I'm so torn about whether to speak up."

It is extremely important, then, for at least

one woman – Dr. Ford, Sally Field, or others who may get into the spotlight, to be willing to come fully into the spotlight in order to show the rest that, no matter what, they have to tell their stories so they too can heal. It is imperative for growth and self-respect to tell someone who will listen (whether it is a lawyer, a supportive friend, a group of women, your sister, whomever it is that can hold your truth), about what you need to say. Do this for your own sake – no one else's.

Once I was staying in a hotel for a meeting, and I noticed it was also the site of a conference. As I watched people scurry about, I stopped a young woman and asked her what the conference was about. "Well," she said, "It's hard to describe. I brought a notebook to fill with this person's wisdom but so far all we've done is sit in silence for two hours. I haven't written a thing in here except insights I had during the meditation." I was astounded that around two hundred people were waiting for someone they had decided was an authority to tell them their truth. The leader was wise enough to turn that task over to the participants.

> The privilege of a lifetime is being
> who you are.
> Sheldon Kopp

For a long time I have kept in mind, due to my own sexual abuse, that a spider spins its web from the center of its being, then stands on it. I have learned, over time, that I know I must stand on who I truly am, not who I wish I were or who I think I can fool about who I want them to think I am. No, I must do it myself about myself – standing on the knowing that that is the only solid ground I have – the center of my own being.

I notice that I speak differently, from this awareness of the foundation of truth within myself. This has created openings for further truths to come forward once I removed that perceived stone that I had allowed to keep me so silent.

Souls are God's jewels, every one of
which is worth many worlds.
Thomas Traherne

Build thee more stately mansions,
O my soul.
Oliver Wendell Holmes

No one can stop our voices now, and no one can halt our knowing that not only do we have a voice, but that we must use it for our own transformation. The social movements about this issue will only get larger over time. There will be other hashtags. What's yours?

I can open to the pain of the world within in confidence that it can neither shatter nor isolate me, for I am not an object that can break. I am a resilient pattern within a vaster web of knowing.
Joanna Macy

CHAPTER 6

Here Comes the Sun

There is a brokenness
out of which comes the unbroken,
a shatteredness
out of which blooms the
unshatterable …
as we break open to the place inside,
which is unbreakable and whole,
while learning to sing.

Rashami

ONE OF MY first awakenings came as I was given the chance to experience a chrysalis turning into a butterfly. The most delicate time for this process was very moving: the chrysalis was hanging by one silk thread, and any movement at the edge of the container would have ruined the possibility of this beautiful butterfly being born. It is one of the most precious memories I have to this day. I invite you to have the same experience if you have the opportunity. It is truly wonderful to observe a miracle unfolding before us. It can also initiate healing because it is truly an invitation to take the time to go into your own woven chrysalis. Allow your spirit to speak to you about what your life has been like up until this point, including being mistreated at some or many points in your life and emerge a butterfly, knowing you will never ever allow that treatment again. It is a kind of rebirth that can occur, and you will experience a freedom you never thought possible.

What was my own process of healing like and how long did it take? It was and, in many ways, still is an ongoing experience, that occurs each time I am confronted by a situation, whether it is a new position in a company, a new relationship, a new city, anything that I haven't encountered before.

Each time I ask myself, what am I going to do with this untoward behavior toward me? Where can I turn for guidance? Who can tell me whether leaving this minute is an appropriate response to the particular harassment and abuse or not? First, I had to turn within myself and ask: "How does this feel to me? Is this behavior familiar in any way?" I took time to ponder exactly what I was feeling and decide what the best choice would be after I expressed my anger in my car, to a friend, and a few other ways.

Later, when I got away from the third man I had dated in a rather short period of time, I decided that I wouldn't date at all for a while. I tell many patients the same thing. The ones who are willing to take the advice say that spending time getting reacquainted with themselves and discovering what they really want for their lives is astounding, the difference it made in their choices. I have them even envision living alone, how they would decorate their place, what they would choose. It was amazing to witness their faces as they described what *they* would choose for themselves. In the process, it became clear to them that they had allowed the other person to have more of a "vote" in the decision-making (and in every other aspect of their lives, including their bodies, their power, their ability to make decisions based on what was best for their own well-being) than they realized. They said, almost under their breath, "Never again."

How would your life change if you took some time away from all your current friends, coworkers, family—not literally perhaps, although a "therapeutic separation" is often exactly what needs to happen. But if this is not possible, at least create some separation in your mind from those to whom you have given the power to identify who you are?

What if you simply stayed with your own thoughts, perceptions, questions you ask yourself, your own predilections, your own decisions? If you have never tried it, you will have no way of answering that question. There is no way to *guess* just what would change. Perhaps nothing would change, perhaps everything would or, of course, something in between. Try it. It is a powerful exercise in getting to know who you are, beyond any outside influence. A wonderful proverb that Bethany McClean quoted in her article in *Vanity Fair* states: "They tried to bury us; they didn't know we were seeds."

Many of you don't realize that your internal world speaks to you throughout the day. Once you have provided it some space so that you can hear it, it will grow and flourish for you. In a way, you are saying to the chatterbox that is your mind's constant stream of thinking, repeated over and over each day, "I must free myself of myself so that the wise soul within me can have its way."

Truly, there is a huge difference between your mind's chatter and the "still, small voice" that yearns to have more space to be heard. That's impossible if first, you don't know you have one and second, you just "don't have time for such foolishness." Let me tell you, that wise place inside you has plenty to say, wisdom you never knew you had. But it won't ever compete for your attention. You need to give it the honor of listening. In truth, it is, of course, meditation.

People say, "I can't seem to get my thoughts to stop in order to meditate." That is very true at first. I invite patients to see the thoughts as clouds floating by. As they come into your awareness, just watch them. Don't give them any attention because then you provide energy for them to keep staying alive and thriving. That is the opposite of what you really want. You want to be still and know that very quiet voice that has deep wisdom to impart to you. One of the great ways I have been able to heal has been to open up a pathway for this soul to lead me instead of my old, worn-out thoughts that have run my life all along.

What can you do to enrich your soul on a continuing basis besides giving it space to speak? Some ways patients have found that worked well for them are things such as gardening several times a week (both men and women have reported how renewing this process is for them), taking off "pointless masks" that really didn't serve them but they wore each day anyway (a habit you have to consciously become aware of), and pursuing new arenas for self-expression. For example, one woman has told me recently that she wants to pursue oil painting. She is very excited about it, and it seems to have brought out a whole new side in her. She went inward instead of turning out into the world to see how she could distract herself. You see, she has gone through great sexual trauma for the last seven months, so this new expression has given her a brand-new perspective on her own life, apart from the immense pain of that trauma. It is inspiring to witness.

So, what are you feeling you might like to undertake as a way of contacting that wise voice deep within you? The world that surrounds you has pulled your attention far away from your inner life—sexual harassment, daily taunting by men in the workplace, invitations you are tempted by but know will lead you into more pain. The internal part of you, though, has so much wisdom (that is only yours) to give you. Making room for it is all that is required of you. At least experiment with listening to that voice; it has always been there, but so many distractions may have kept you from even thinking about allowing it space. Now's the time.

Rainer Maria Rilke stated in the *Letters on Life* that "no rejection, no hardship, no insults are entirely without prospects—the densest shrub can yield leaves, a flower, a fruit ..." How have your own inappropriate experiences deepened you? Have you let them yet? They can change you, open you, and expand you. Rilke said, "Where something becomes extremely difficult and unbearable, there we also stand always already quite near our own transformation."

We are ripe for that transformation when we are into our deepest pain or despair. I know that because I experienced it, and I have seen it with numerous patients over the years.

What I think happens to those of us with experiences of horribly inappropriate insults, remarks, or behavior is that it pushes us more deeply into life, our lives, and life itself. It demands of us the most extreme growth into our own ever-increasing strengths. Have you noticed that at all yet? What exactly have *you* learned about yourself through these extremely inappropriate experiences of harassment or mistreatment? Have you become more aware of your feelings, more sensitive toward yourself and others, and more self-loving? If not, then it is time to begin taking note of how you can move in that direction—toward great growth experiences that truly make a huge difference in the quality of your life.

When Iyanla Vanzant wrote a book called *Until Today*, she stated that "The greatest service I can offer myself is the elimination of my own self-doubt." She added, "Know what you know about you without trying to gain support or validation from others." It is as if she had read my mind and written what I've been sharing with you. Truly, though, we get into trouble, lots of trouble, when we want something, anything, from another because it becomes a set-up for inappropriate comments or worse behavior and insidious mistreatment.

Ernest Holmes wrote in *This Thing Called Life* that we must say, "I am greater than the sum total of all the experiences I have had. I can heal from (whatever it is) for I am strong, must be in a deep connection with that (still small voice) because it has all the wisdom, intelligence and guidance we need. We must learn to resurrect ourselves." That last sentence is the most powerful one to me—what a phrase; what a concept. Please consider incorporating that phrase into your thinking.

"Doctor, I had the most amazing experience last night. I could hardly wait to get here. I have never let myself be what I would call 'out of control.' I mean, I was never comfortable with not being in control—in business, in relationships or anywhere really, as you know. I have taken great advantage of women, too, as part of being in control. I have sexually abused them when they really didn't want to have sex with me. Now I see that I needed to feel I could just take them because I was stronger and more in power and over them with power. Afterwards, though, I never felt good about it and of course was never able to get them to have a date with me again. I know you have suggested that I do a certain experiment, but I never had the urge even to bother trying it. Last week, though, after I left your office I decided to at least give it a try. Well, for a week now I have been getting up at 4:30 instead of 5:30 each morning. I go into my garden room right off my library, and I focus on one particular flower. I look at it, experience the beauty of it, and eventually I can just stare at it with no thoughts about it, or anything else for that matter. I watch my thoughts, as we talked about, but I don't stay with any of them. That has helped me the most. Eventually, they stop on their own.

Anyway, back to last night. I went into the garden room and decided to calm myself from the turmoil I'd experienced. I am concerned about how quickly I am evolving out of my old controlling ways. But, last night, I was sitting in that room and I felt this loosening of the hold I have felt about who I am. I sensed a weakening of the notion that I am only and irrevocably 'John' who does this and that. I began to see that 'John' is an object, a role, rather than the sum total of who I am. I am so much more than that small image I had of me that I am astounded."

This patient, whom I had been seeing for quite a while, suddenly saw what we had been working on for many months. It was his own willingness to keep doing what he had promised himself he would do. He reaped the rewards on that day and the next and the next. He could never go back to that old "John" who had to control everything. What a new beginning for him. He was committed to therapy and did what it took to move him to where he had wanted to be—not when he entered the office, but when he realized just how much effort and energy it took for him to keep doing what he had been doing. Besides, he didn't like himself anymore the way he had been; he just didn't know a way out.

Emmanuel says it so well in his second book (called *Book Two*): "Thought is a tool to take you to the gate. Then you must leave your tools behind." When I read this quote, I thought, yes, we have grown up with so many tools we have used to "get by," but those tools could only take us to where we have been many times in our lives; they can't get us to brand-new places we haven't yet experienced. That comes with letting go of them, putting on a "new set of clothes," so to speak, a style we've never worn before. "Hey, it looks kinda good. I think I'll go out in these today, try on this new look."

> Every process involves breaking
> something up
> The earth must be broken to bring
> forth life.

If the seed does not die, there is no
plant.
Bread results from the death of wheat.
Joseph Campbell

I'd like you to, in your mind, say an answer to this statement: "If I do not stand for something, I will fall for anything." To me, that is a very poignant set of words that conveys to me that we must stand for our own lives, for our own thoughts, our own power, our own hegemony over ourselves. That is a critical step to overcoming being a part of the group who is *not* willing to be a participant in the #MeToo movement. It was startling and astounding to hear Stormy Daniels say in the interview she did with Anderson Cooper in March 2018 that she was not a part of the #MeToo movement because she didn't think of herself and didn't want to think of herself as a "victim."

I don't know about you, but for me, standing with all the women who have come forward, including all those gymnasts who spoke up at the trial against Dr. Larry Nassar who had treated and sexually abused them for so many years, as very brave women who had the courage to say *enough, never again, how dare you* and so on with whatever phrases they said when they spoke about their experiences. They were hardly being a victim to it, but rather, these women had become so *done* with the mistreatment and swallowing their power that they had to say something. All the women who speak up (including me) are still saying something now. The movement is far from over, and women everywhere are gaining the courage to say what they have experienced. Sometimes it takes a few very brave women to speak out. Then others begin to think, "Hmmm, have I had that experience too?" Often, the answer is yes.

> …and then the day came when the risk to remain tight in a bud was more painful than the risk it took to blossom.
> **Anais Nin**

CHAPTER 7

Twist and Shout

My barn burned to the ground.

Now I can see the moon.

J. Stone

THE MORE YOU nurture your Soul, the more It can nurture you. You are now transcending that old space you used to inhabit and thus can bring a new perspective to everything you do, say, and choose to experience. You are awakening; it is a process, but truly, you are no longer sound asleep. You have become conscious of what is happening around you and have the ability (and, I trust, the willingness) to question whether it seems (and thus is) appropriate for you in terms of respect, fair treatment, and whether you have truly been listened to, not just endured until *they* (whoever "they" are) can get back to their own agenda. Author William T. Bridges put it succinctly: "Genuine beginnings begin within us, even when they are brought to us by external opportunities."

You must not join the movement because you think it is important to be part of a popular group. It won't work for you in the process of really having you deepen your understanding of what your own experience of mistreatment has been. Often, I encourage my patients to write in a journal every day—not recording what they did that day but deeply getting in touch with what they felt as they went through the day. Ask yourself: Did I feel heard? Did I feel respected? Did anyone dishonor me? What was my overall experience today? Do I feel appreciated for who I am, not just for what I do? Many questions such as these will assist you in going deeper into the journaling process. You will be surprised at what you write, especially the more you do it on a regular basis.

It is really time now for you to move into a new phase of your life—to shout from the window or door or car as you drive: "This is me! I don't have to please you to be me. I just get to choose to be me." So much of the research I did spoke of how we must get angry, enraged about what has happened to us throughout so many years. We can't be silenced anymore, or it damages us. It eats away even more now, since we know what has been happening to us. So, that isn't an option.

We do shout, we do kick rocks, branches, anything that we can find to express, to act out (with inanimate objects) the absolute fire inside of us that has been burning for many years. Until now, we didn't know what to do with it or that we could actually do something about it. First there is getting the anger out in all the ways we can think of that feels good and doesn't harm you or another person.

What a feeling, what joy emerges when you actually take the time to twist out of that old form and move into the you that you've envisioned at some point you could be. It *does* take bravery, it *does* take willingness and most of all it *does* take time to grow into that new image of who and what you decide you are going to be from this moment on. That would be a great thing to write about in a journal. Get to know who that person is, what she thinks, how she thinks, what she feels, without anyone telling you how you are to feel or pleasing someone so they will accept you. Do you realize how much time you've already spent doing that?

I sometimes become very upset when I think about all I did to attempt to get attention and acceptance. I thought I needed it from these people, in order to feel worthy to breathe! Too long; it was exhausting and never got me what I thought I had to have. It is like what Taylor Swift said in that trial: "I am not going to let you or your client make me feel in any way that it is my fault." The most important point she makes, though, is when she says that what this DJ did was a product of *his* decisions. What a powerful notion that is, to know completely that nothing you did or could do or will do caused the insidious mistreatment you received. Put the blame back where it belongs, with this man, whoever he is. It has nothing to do with you; it is his hunger for power, his need for control, his obsession with getting away with placing you in a "one down" position so he can feel that omnipotence he thinks he needs. Who cares what he wants, though? It is your body, your life, your self-worth, and you will never let any man dare to attempt in any way to get you to turn that over, even for a minute, to him or anyone else anymore. It is your body, your life, and your decisions now that are sacred, to be held in that way forever.

Yes, it is a new day for you. You can decide if you have to have that kind of man I've been discussing or those people in order to go on. Let me tell you—you don't. *You* must come to that conclusion yourself, though. No one can convince you of that, especially since it has probably been many years that you have yearned for that acceptance—in the way you thought you needed it—to feel whole. If what you are doing now hasn't materialized into the achievement of your wishes, hopes, and dreams, it most likely won't. Obviously, you aren't going to go out the first day and shout from the window, "No more, I'm through!" It doesn't happen that quickly, but if you keep walking in the direction that you know is going to eventually provide you with more self-respect, more of a sense of power about yourself and the world, more of a knowing that, not only do you have a voice, but that voice (you) have something to say, then gradually, without even realizing it, you will have grown into a new way of being.

There is some mystery about what causes a person to make that first step toward healthy change. If discomfort were enough, then our childhoods, after the first few years, would have been different. But they weren't. They weren't because of the word *hope*. We just hoped that things would get better, not by some magic but by the people we were living with waking up to why we were so unhappy or so quiet, or however it manifested for you in your home. Alas, that most likely didn't happen back then. Sometimes it only happens when there is a critical mass of people, mostly women, who have the courage to speak out for what they know is mistreatment. Then, perhaps you begin to wonder if maybe you had some mistreatment that you never named, along the way to adulthood.

What I have found, with my patients as well as my own journey, is that once they (and I) got a taste of what change felt like, we embraced it. It was no longer so scary to become what we were to be all along, a person with self-worth, a sense of hegemony over our lives, a feeling that we did have power in the world, but we'd just never been willing to go toward it. Once you taste it, you will likely never go back to allowing the mistreatment, the put-downs, the harassment, the disrespect that plagued your life. Suddenly, it seemed, there were more opportunities opening up to practice the "new you." What a concept, especially if you'd never ever had the experience.

Of course, life is always about choices—choices that can either further us in this life journey or hold us back. Choices can open doors or close them. They can enhance our power or deplete our power, create immense happiness or cause us sorrow. Naturally, choices were not something we felt (rightfully so, I think) as children. Some of this lack of a sense of any power took a toll on the ways we felt about ourselves. Now it is different, though, and we must, if we are going to move forward, pick those choices that enrich and bless us.

You may have heard often, "Speak truth to power." I say, "Speak *up* with power."

I wrote this poem a few years ago, as I was in the early part of my process of consecrating my inner realm, the space where my Soul lives. I was moved to offer a tribute to the connection I have always felt with nature because, more than anything else, it taught me many important lessons about life as well as nurtured that inner life I was getting so close with. Nature also dependably offered me a way to connect with it, a way to honor it:

I am the Wave
that sparks the ocean shore,
pushing inward and outward
at the same moment,
finding Its own rhythm,
Its own Truth.

I am the Sun,
making diamonds of that blue,
magnificent sea,
Lighting the way
through all the darkness
To the only Presence there is.

I am the Moon,
reflecting its own Soul back

onto Itself, to learn to grow, to be,
to stay forever within Its own Oneness.

I am that Flower, wanting to live, to
show Its beauty, Its divinity, only
by Being, never by performing.

It is only Itself,
this Ocean Wave, this Sun, this
Moon, this Flower,
never trying to imitate,
never wanting to compete.

All work perfectly
because they stayed in their own
brilliant Essence
their own
Spiritual Home.

ABOUT THE AUTHOR

LUCY PAPILLON PH.D. is a clinical psychol-

ogist in private prac-
tice in Hermosa Beach
and Beverly Hills,
California. She has
served on the faculty at
UCI Medical School,
authored two books,

and appeared as an expert in numerous publica-
tions. Dr. Papillon currently lectures throughout
the United States and the world. For more about
her, visit www.drpapillon.com.